LAND OF THE FREE

FREEDOM OF ASSEMBLY

By
David C. King

THE MILLBROOK PRESS
Brookfield, Connecticut

Published by The Millbrook Press, Inc.
2 Old New Milford Road
Brookfield, CT 06804
© 1997 Blackbirch Graphics, Inc.

5 4 3 2 1

Created and produced in association with Blackbirch Graphics.
Series Editor: Tanya Lee Stone
Editor: Lisa Clyde Nielsen
Associate Editor: Elizabeth M. Taylor
Production Editor: Laura Specht Patchkofsky

Photo credits
Cover and page 6: Photodisc; pp. 5, 21, 38: ©Blackbirch Press, Inc.; pp. 8,
12, 25, 30, 41: AP/Wide World Photos, Inc.; p. 11: ©Johnson/Gamma
Liaison; pp. 13, 32: Collection of the Supreme Court of the United States;
pp. 15, 16, 20, 26: Library of Congress; pp. 19, 22: North Wind Picture
Archives; p. 27: ©Frank Wolfe/LBJ Library Collection; p. 28: ©Michael
Abramson/Gamma Liaison; p. 33: ©Ralf-Finn Hestoft/SABA; p. 35:
©Benali/Liaison USA; p. 36: ©Brad Markel/Gamma Liaison; p. 37:
©Gifford/Liaison USA; p. 43: ©James Leynse/SABA.

Library of Congress Cataloging-in-Publication Data

King, David C.
Freedom of assembly / David C. King.
p. cm. — (Land of the free)
Includes bibliographical references and index.
Summary: Focuses on freedom of assembly and its close link to
freedom of expression as guaranteed by the Bill of Rights.
ISBN 0-7613-0064-3 (lib. ed.)
1. Assembly, Right of—United States—Juvenile literature. 2.
Freedom of speech—United States—Juvenile literature. 3.
Demonstrations—United States—Juvenile literature.
[1. Assembly, Right of. 2. Freedom of speech.] I. Title.
II. Series: Land of the free (Brookfield, Conn.)
KF4778.Z9K56 1997
342.73'0853—dc20
[347.302853] 96-21960 CIP AC

Contents

Introduction

★ ★ ★ ★ ★ ★ ★ ★ ★ ★

Suppose that you could be arrested for reading a book, going to church, or talking with your friends. Sound impossible? Not everywhere. Your rights to do all these things, and many others, are guaranteed under U.S. law. But people in many other countries have no such guarantees. Their governments tell them what they may and may not read, write, and say, what religion they must follow, and even how they should vote—that is, if they are allowed to vote at all.

Americans are proud of their freedoms. Even so, many Americans don't know very much about those freedoms, or about the responsibilities that come with them. It is important to understand your rights, so that you can use them—and defend them.

The books in the *Land of the Free* series tell you about our most important American rights and freedoms: the right to speak freely, to vote in elections, to worship as we choose, and to join with others who share our views and goals. Most of these rights are set out in the U.S. Constitution and its first ten amendments, the Bill of Rights.

The Constitution and the Bill of Rights were written more than 200 years ago, soon after the United States won its independence from Britain. The authors of the Constitution believed that freedom would flourish under democracy. A democratic government, elected by the people, serves the people—not the other way around. Many of the rights in the Constitution help guarantee that democracy will continue.

The authors of the Constitution broke new ground, creating a society that valued and respected liberty. Over the years, adapting to changes in society, Americans have re-interpreted and expanded the rights that the country's founders set out. Yet, the basic principles behind those rights have not changed, and they apply just as well today as they did 200 years ago. Only if we understand how our freedoms work, and why they are essential, will they continue to flourish for years to come.

• The Constitution's First Amendment grants every American
the right to assemble with others in a peaceful way.

Chapter 1

"PEACEABLY TO ASSEMBLE..."

The first glimpse of America for millions of newcomers has been the Statue of Liberty. The statue is a symbol of what our nation stands for: a nation governed by "We the people." Its government was created to provide order and to protect the individual liberties, or freedoms, of its people.

Five of the most important freedoms are spelled out in the First Amendment to the U.S. Constitution: freedom of religion, speech, the press, assembly, and petition. The amendment states:

> *"Congress shall make no law respecting an establishment of religion, or prohibiting the free exercise thereof; or abridging the freedom of speech, or of the press, or the right of the people peaceably to assemble, and to petition the government for a redress of grievances."*

In this book, we will take a look at the right of assembly.

"The right of the people peaceably to assemble" simply means that people may gather in groups for whatever purpose they choose. Americans join together—or assemble—in all sorts of groups every day, from Boy or Girl Scouts to the United States Senate. They also meet in many informal groups—a school picnic, a group of friends watching television, or church members holding a baked goods sale.

Why do individuals need a special statement in the Constitution to protect their freedom of assembly? Part of the answer can be found in the phrase, "to petition the government for a redress of grievances." Those words are designed to protect people who have assembled because they are unhappy with the government. These people may assemble in hope that their concerns are addressed.

Here is an example of how Americans in one community have exercised their rights of assembly and petition:

When a community bands together for a cause, it can often be a powerful force for change.

In the spring of 1994, the residents of a New Jersey housing project were upset when a law was passed banning parking on the streets of the project. People would have to use a city parking lot located two blocks away. They would also have to pay a fee.

Some of the residents said, "Well, that's the law. We can't do anything about it." But other residents knew that there was a lot they could do. They met to plan how to solve their problem. In organizing this meeting, they were exercising their constitutional right of assembly. At the meeting, some people said that they had written letters to the mayor and to the city council stating their opposition to the new law. These letters were actually a form of petition, asking the government to help them with their grievance.

The residents voted to draw up a more formal petition. They wrote a list of reasons why they felt that the parking law was unfair and should be changed. Then they set up tables in the lobby of each project building so that other residents could read a copy of the petition and sign their names if they agreed with it. This form of petition would show that a large number of people opposed the law.

Those attending the project meeting considered one other plan of action. The plan was to hold a public protest rally, or demonstration, in front of City Hall. Some people offered to make signs declaring that the mayor and the city council were being unfair. The demonstration would be another type of assembly, another way to appeal to the city government to make a change. As it turned out, the demonstration was not needed. After receiving the petitions, the city council agreed to reconsider the parking law.

The people of the housing project provided a living example of how American government is designed to work. The citizens of a democracy have a voice in their own lives, beyond electing representatives to speak for them.

The rights of assembly are closely related to freedom of speech. A private or public gathering of people offers an opportunity to share information and ideas. It is also a time to speak out when people feel that the government is not acting in the people's interest.

Protecting individual rights is particularly important for any group whose cause is opposed by the majority of people or by the government. Many of the important changes in American society began with small groups insisting on and defending their rights—especially their rights to freedom of assembly, petition, speech, and the press. In earlier times, and in many other countries even today, these groups would not have been allowed to freely express their views.

Defining Freedom's Limits

The First Amendment states, in part: "Congress shall make no law...abridging [limiting]...the right of the people peaceably to assemble, and to petition the government for a redress of grievances." That statement is very general. It does not say what those rights are or how they apply in different situations. Most people agree that there have to be some limits to every freedom. Freedom of speech, for

example, does not mean that someone can encourage others to riot. And a group blocking a busy intersection is not exercising a legal right of assembly because it would be interfering with the rights of others.

Because the First Amendment does not spell out exactly what the freedoms mean in every situation, certain historical events have forced the Supreme Court to define the subtle applications of the First Amendment rights bit by bit. Has a meeting or demonstration interfered with the rights of others? Does a certain law unfairly limit people's right to assemble and petition?

A 1993 case involving the picketing of a radio station shows how a dispute involving freedom of assembly was settled in court:

A group of people in New York City were angry about a radio talk show. The show's host used foul language and said ugly things about people who belonged to racial

Americans can use their right of free assembly to voice their dissatisfaction about political issues.

minorities. The group decided to protest by marching with picket signs in front of the office building where the radio station was located. But people in the office building complained that the protesters were blocking the entrance to the building. After several warnings by police, the protesters were arrested.

In court, the protesters claimed that they were merely exercising their right to assemble peaceably. It was up to the judge to decide if the arrest violated their rights. The judge ruled against the protesters. The picketers, she said, were interfering with the rights of others to enter or leave the building.

In general, the exercise of any freedom can be limited if it interferes with the rights of others, or if it represents a danger to public safety.

After a court decides, or rules, on a case, the losing side may appeal the decision—that is, it may ask to be heard by a higher court. A few cases are appealed all the way to

Soldiers break up anti-Vietnam war protesters who tried to enter the Pentagon in 1967.

the U.S. Supreme Court, the nation's highest court. The decision of the nine Supreme Court justices is final. They have the last word in deciding how to apply the Constitution to each and every particular situation.

When a case involving a basic right, such as freedom of assembly, reaches the Supreme Court, the justices try very hard to uphold that right. At the same time, they know that the government must be allowed to make laws to preserve public order and safety. But they insist that any restrictions be limited, clearly stated, and applied fairly to everyone.

For example, in 1969, in the city of Birmingham, Alabama, a law was passed making it a crime for people to assemble on a city sidewalk after being asked to move by police officers. When several African Americans were arrested for violating this law, they appealed their convictions. Eventually, the case reached the Supreme Court.

The justices of the Supreme Court shown here in 1993, have the last word in legal matters concerning the Constitution.

The Court ruled that Birmingham's law was unconstitutional because it was not clear in stating what kind of behavior was being prohibited. Instead, the law left it up to the police officers to decide whether or not a gathering was illegal. The danger in this kind of law, the justices said, was that the police could arrest members of any group they didn't like or who represented ideas that the police opposed.

Making Change Possible

The Constitution of the United States has worked well for more than 200 years. One reason for this success is that the document is amazingly flexible. As times have changed and new needs have arisen, Congress and the courts have found new ways to apply the broad statements of the Constitution and the Bill of Rights to every situation.

Many important changes in our nation have been brought about by people exercising their right to assemble and to petition the federal government. When the Constitution was written, for example, women did not have the right to vote. They were denied many other rights as well. Beginning in the 1830s, a few women began holding meetings to talk about what they could do to win their full rights as citizens. Over the years, more meetings were held, often attended by men who agreed with the cause. Petitions were sent to Congress, urging that the Constitution be amended to grant women the right to vote. Marches and demonstrations were held, and women carried banners demanding their rights.

Finally, with the passage of the Nineteenth Amendment in 1920, after nearly a century of struggle, women won the right to vote.

Through all those years of protest and petition, the women who took part in this movement were protected by the First Amendment. The men who controlled the government were able to deny women the right to vote, but they could not deny women the right to assemble peaceably and to petition the government.

As you will see in the next chapter, other important changes have come about because people have had the right to assemble. In fact, the very creation of the United States as an independent nation depended on the freedom that people have to assemble and work together toward a common goal.

Peaceful protest has accomplished much in the past. Here, in 1913, women march for the right to vote.

• The need for the right to free assembly was made clear just before the Revolution. Here, colonists gather to protest the Stamp Act, which eventually helped incite people to war.

Chapter 2

THE EVOLUTION OF
FREEDOM OF ASSEMBLY

Before the American Revolution, the thirteen American colonies were part of Britain's overseas empire. The English law-making body—Parliament—and the king allowed the colonists to govern most of their own affairs. Each colony had its own assembly and a governor, who was usually appointed by the king.

The system worked well for more than a century. The colonies grew larger and became prosperous. The people of the colonies considered themselves English citizens and loyal subjects of the king or queen. But after 1760, the colonists were troubled by some of the laws passed by Parliament. They especially disliked the taxes that they were now being forced to pay. The colonists had no representatives in Parliament, so they had no voice in even deciding what those taxes would be.

Without representatives in Parliament, it was hard for the colonists to let England know why they objected to these taxes and other new laws. But they believed in their right to assemble to discuss problems and to petition the government to address those problems. When Parliament and the king ignored their petitions, the colonists became increasingly frustrated. After 1765, the conflict between the colonies and England steadily grew worse. The colonists felt they had no choice but to openly rebel.

One of the tax laws that most outraged the colonists was the Stamp Act, passed in 1765. This law required colonists to pay taxes on anything that was printed, such as newspapers and other documents. Angry colonists responded by calling an assembly of delegates (represen- tatives) from all the colonies. The delegates to this Stamp Act Congress wrote a Declaration of Rights and Grievances. The declaration explained the reasons why the stamp tax was unfair. It stated "that it is the right of the British subjects in these colonies to petition the king...or Parliament."

Parliament finally agreed to remove the stamp tax, but it soon insisted on creating new taxes. This made the problem even worse. In 1774, another meeting of dele- gates was called. This meeting became known as the First Continental Congress. The delegates issued a "Declaration of Resolves" stating that "...their dutiful, humble, loyal, and reasonable petitions...for redress have been repeatedly treated with contempt." The Congress appealed to Parliament and the king to respect the colonists' rights.

The Magna Carta

For many centuries, England was ruled by kings or queens who had complete authority over the people. As subjects of these powerful rulers, the people had no voice in how they were governed. Anyone who dared to speak out against royal authority was banished, imprisoned, or killed.

Then, in 1215, a group of nobles forced King John to sign a document called the Magna Carta, or "Great Charter." The document gave the nobles certain rights. For example, the king could no longer tax them without their consent. And, if there were any grievances against the king in the future, the nobles "shall petition to have it redressed without delay." Although later kings sometimes ignored these provisions, the Magna Carta provided the foundation for constitutional government in England.

The Magna Carta had applied to only the most powerful nobles. The extension of these rights to all English citizens developed slowly over several hundred years. More than 400 years later, another landmark was achieved when Parliament passed England's Bill of Rights in 1689. This Bill of Rights made it clear that there were limits to royal authority, and it guaranteed the basic liberties of the English people. Among the rights protected from the government was "the right of the subjects to petition the king."

American colonists, like the people of England itself, cherished these rights. It was when the rights seemed threatened by Parliament and the king that the colonists felt justified in launching the American Revolution.

King John signs the Magna Carta.

England responded by clamping down harder. It even planned to use military force to control its colonists. The colonists now felt that they had no choice but to fight for their rights. This fight would soon become the American Revolution. The first battles of the American Revolution were fought in the spring of 1775. Even then, a Second Continental Congress tried one last time to petition King George III. The king, however, refused even to read the document. A few months later, the Congress issued the powerful Declaration of Independence, transforming the thirteen colonies into the 13 states of a new nation.

In explaining why the colonies were forming an independent nation, the Declaration stated that "in every stage of [the king's] oppressions we have petitioned for redress." But every petition was "answered only by repeated injury." The Declaration went on to explain the fundamental idea of democracy: All people have certain God-given rights. Governments are created to protect those rights. When a government fails to do this, the people have the right to overthrow the government and establish a new one.

While Americans were fighting a war to win their independence, people in each of the states wrote new state constitutions. These replaced their colonial charters from England. Most of the states' constitutions included a bill of rights, listing the individual

Delegates and representatives arrive at a meeting of the First Continental Congress in 1774.

liberties that the government could not take away. These liberties included freedom of assembly and petition, along with such other basic freedoms as freedom of speech, the press, and religion.

When the United States Constitution was written in 1787 to create a strong central government, Americans remembered how Parliament and the king had abused their rights, disbanded assemblies, and ignored petitions. They insisted that these rights receive special protection in the Bill of Rights, which were the first ten amendments added to the federal Constitution in 1791.

The Declaration of Independence set the stage for the ideas and rights set forth in the U.S. Constitution.

Exercising the Right of Assembly

During the nineteenth century, the First Amendment provided protection for several important reform movements. In addition to the movement for women's voting rights, discussed in Chapter 1, abolitionists—Americans who opposed slavery—began holding large-scale meetings in the 1830s. Men and women, whites, and free African Americans joined together to demand that the government abolish (eliminate) slavery in the states of the South. So many petitions were sent to the government that in 1840, Congress passed a "gag rule," which said that no more anti-slavery petitions could be read aloud in the Senate. However, except for that limitation, Congress did not interfere with the right of anti-slavery groups to assemble or to speak and write about the need to abolish slavery.

At the same time, though, the national government did nothing to protect people at anti-slavery meetings from *local* actions and laws. In many communities, abolitionists were attacked by mobs or arrested for "disturbing the peace." The Supreme Court took no action because it felt that the First Amendment offered protection only for laws passed by Congress, not for local or state laws.

A similar thing happened in the late 1800s. Industrial workers began forming large labor unions to improve working conditions and workers' pay. The national government allowed the states and communities to regulate union meetings and activities. When unions called strikes (work stoppages) to demand higher wages or better working conditions, local police were ordered to break up the strikes. More than 500 strikes were ended when state governors called out the militia to force workers back on the job. Finally, in 1933, the workers won recognition of their right to strike.

Anti-slavery protests played an important role in abolishing slavery.

The Denial of Free Assembly in America

In countries controlled by powerful rulers, people have often been denied the right to assemble. In some countries, even meetings in people's homes have been forbidden. The reason for this tight control has been the fear that any meeting might lead to a discussion of grievances against the government. If people cannot meet in groups, the governments have reasoned, they cannot plan a rebellion.

The same fear of rebellion fueled harsh laws limiting the rights of African-American slaves in the United States during the 1800s. For example, an early law in Virginia stated that "the frequent meeting of considerable numbers of negro [black] slaves under pretense of feasts and burials is judged dangerous and should be forbidden." During the nineteenth century, up to the Civil War (1861–1865), armed militia in the South patrolled slave quarters "and other places suspected of entertaining unlawful assemblies."

The outlawing of slavery by President Abraham Lincoln during the Civil War finally won for African Americans the rights of citizenship, including the right to free assembly.

All of these early and important reform movements depended on "...the right of the people peaceably to assemble, and to petition the government for a redress of grievances."

The right to assemble in large public demonstrations, such as marches and protest rallies, was also vital to the civil rights movement that began in the late 1950s. Large groups of African Americans, often joined by sympathetic whites, gathered to protest injustices. They rallied against state and local laws in the South that prevented blacks from voting and established racially segregated (separate) schools and other public facilities.

On March 2, 1961, for example, 187 students held a demonstration in Columbia, South Carolina. In orderly groups of 15, they marched from a church to the grounds of the State Capitol. Some carried signs with slogans like, "Down With Segregation," and "I am Proud to be a Negro." After 45 minutes, police officers ordered them to leave. Instead, the young people stayed, singing religious and patriotic songs. They were arrested for "disturbing the peace." They were tried in court, found guilty, and ordered to pay fines.

Some of the students appealed their convictions. When the case, *Edwards* v. *South Carolina*, finally reached the Supreme Court in 1963, the justices reversed the convictions. The Court ruled that a peaceful assembly held on public property was protected by the First Amendment, as long as the group did not disturb the peace in some way that was a danger to others.

In making decisions about public assemblies, the Supreme Court has been careful to protect private property and public safety. A large demonstration, no matter how peaceful, cannot take place on private property, and it cannot represent a possible danger to others or to public well-being. In 1963, for instance, a group of Florida students held a peaceful demonstration. They were protesting the arrest of other African-American demonstrators. But this time, the students assembled on jail property. The

Supreme Court ruled that the demonstrators could be arrested and fined because the students were on private property. The Court's decision stated that people who want to hold a public demonstration "do not have a constitutional right to do it whenever and however and wherever they please."

The civil rights demonstrators of the 1950s and 1960s were inspired by the leadership of Reverend Martin Luther King, Jr. It was King who encouraged African Americans to confront racial segregation laws by holding large-scale but peaceful demonstrations. In April 1963, for instance, he led a protest march through the streets of Birmingham, Alabama. There were hundreds of marchers, including many young children. The police arrested dozens of demonstrators, and they used fire hoses and police dogs to break up the march. People throughout the nation were horrified by television pictures of these brutal scenes. The federal government moved troops close to the city, demanding that King and his followers be allowed their right to assemble and to petition the government. The city and state restored order and agreed to end most forms of segregation in the city.

Martin Luther King, Jr., was one of the strongest advocates of peaceful protest.

Throughout the South, others followed King's example. By the end of 1963, more than 900 protest demonstrations had been held in 11 southern states. A total of 20,000 protesters were arrested, and many encountered violence. But their exercise of freedom of assembly and petition began to tear down the walls of segregation.

On August 28, 1963, more than 200,000 people—whites and African Americans together—joined King and other civil rights leaders in a "March on Washington for Jobs and Freedom." King delivered his most famous and moving speech—"I Have a Dream"— to the huge gathering in the nation's capital. He urged the nation to live up to its ideal that "All men are created equal."

In the spring of 1965, King led hundreds in a protest march for voting rights in Alabama. Again, the demonstrators encountered police violence. Many were beaten

The massive "March on Washington" was a landmark in the civil rights movement.

and arrested. Finally, with army troops protecting them, 25,000 people completed the march to the state capital. King declared:

We march in the name of the Constitution, knowing that the Constitution is on our side. The right of the people peaceably to assemble and to petition the Government for a redress of grievances shall not be abridged. That's the First Amendment.

President Lyndon B. Johnson responded to King and the civil rights movement by urging Congress to pass the Voting Rights Act of 1965. The new law included measures to make sure that all American citizens could exercise their right to vote. In his speech urging passage of the law, Johnson praised the courage and determination of African Americans. "Their demonstrations have been designed to provoke change, to stir reform," he declared. Through their exercise of the right of assembly and petition, African Americans had "awakened the conscience of this nation."

The 1960s also witnessed demonstrations against the Vietnam War. When officials in one town refused to allow an antiwar march, a judge ordered that the permit be granted. The march, the judge stated, "is a constitutional exercise of freedom of assembly and petition. No matter how unpopular...a viewpoint is, peaceable assembly to express that viewpoint cannot be a crime."

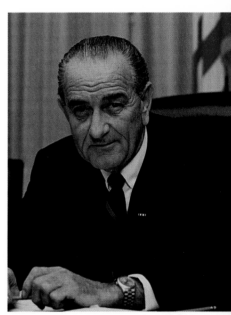

President Lyndon Johnson was influential in getting the Voting Rights Act of 1965 passed by Congress.

• The dramatic power of public assembly is one of the most effective tools of protest Americans can use.

Chapter 3

PROTECTING OUR FREEDOMS

The rights of free assembly and petition involve the expression of ideas. People meet or hold demonstrations to express their views about important issues. People gathered in an auditorium to hear a speech, for example, are exercising both freedom of assembly and freedom of speech. The famous March on Washington in 1963, with speeches by Martin Luther King, Jr., and others, involved both of these freedoms. It was also a petition to the government for a redress of grievances.

What about an assembly of people whose purpose is to spread hatred or destroy democracy? Would such a meeting be protected by the First Amendment? Or could the government order the meeting stopped and perhaps arrest the leaders?

In 1977, a public gathering of Nazis in Chicago, Illinois, sparked debate about the right of free assembly.

The American people and the nation's courts have faced these questions a number of times. One of the most explosive cases occured in 1977, when the American Nazi party applied for a permit to march through the streets of Skokie, Illinois. American Nazis are admirers of Adolf Hitler, whose Nazi party ruled Germany from 1933 to the end of World War II in 1945. Nazis waged a vicious campaign of mass murder against Jews and other ethnic groups that came to be known as the Holocaust.

The people of Skokie were horrified at news of the American Nazi party's plan for a march through their streets. The small city's population included 40,000 Jews, many of whom had survived the Holocaust. City officials searched for a way to refuse a permit to march. They passed a law prohibiting demonstrators from wearing military-style uniforms, and another law against distributing hate literature. When the Nazis planned a rally to protest these laws, the county court ruled that they could not hold the rally.

The Nazis appealed to the courts, claiming that they were being denied freedom of assembly and freedom of expression. The long court battle drew nationwide attention. The American people took part in debating the central question: Did the First Amendment protect a hate group like the Nazis, or did a community have the right to prohibit them from marching?

Many people argued that the First Amendment was not intended to protect people who want to destroy democracy or to deprive others of their rights. Others insisted that the First Amendment protects all groups, no matter how unpopular, as long as they are peaceable. They asked, if the government could deny freedom of assembly and expression to one group, what would prevent it from denying freedoms to other groups? A Jewish civil rights worker said, "The First Amendment has to be for everyone—or someday it will be for no one. That's what happened in Nazi Germany."

In June 1977, the Illinois Supreme Court ruled that the American Nazi party had a right to march. One year

Justice Oliver Wendell Holmes supported the right to express one's beliefs, no matter how offensive they may be.

later, the Nazis held two rallies, but decided to march in Chicago rather than Skokie. The march was met by thousands of angry people, who held a counter-demonstration. More than 2,000 police officers were needed to protect the marchers on both sides.

The courts recognized that protecting basic liberties for all individuals and groups is vital to democracy. Although the judges were sympathetic to the people of Skokie, they knew that the principles of the Constitution must be upheld. More than 50 years earlier, Justice Oliver Wendell Holmes, Jr., had explained it this way: "Our Constitution protects the principle of free thought—not free thought for those who agree with us but freedom for the thought we hate."

The issue of the rights of hate groups and other unpopular groups has continued in the 1990s. Troublesome questions have been raised by the formation of groups that are opposed to the government. These so-called "patriot organizations" have few members, but they have aroused public concern, for several reasons.

Many of these groups, called militias, are heavily armed. They also hold regular military-style maneuvers. They insist that these activities are protected by the Second Amendment, which they believe gives them the right to bear arms, and by the First Amendment right to freedom of assembly. Some members of these groups believe that the great enemy of the American people is the U.S. government. They urge Americans to arm themselves and prepare for war—war against their own government! Another reason for concern about these groups is the possible threat of violence. Many people have come to feel that they are a danger to society. Concern grew after people believed to be linked to militias blew up a federal office building in Oklahoma City in 1995.

What should be done? Should the government pass new laws to prohibit such groups from meeting or from holding military-style maneuvers? While the organizations

The recent growth of anti-government militias has raised concern about possible limits of freedom of assembly.

do encourage people to arm themselves and be prepared to fight, they do not always encourage acts of violence. In fact, most of the organizations have expelled members who talk of committing terrorist acts.

Government agencies monitor the activities of the militias, and arrests are made when laws are broken. In July 1995, members of one group were arrested for possessing illegal weapons. Generally, however, government officials want to avoid raiding any organization's meeting simply because the group's views are anti-government. Such a police raid would be unconstitutional unless a specific law had been broken. Government officials, therefore, are in the position of protecting the First Amendment rights of groups who consider them the enemy.

Freedom of Association

Suppose the girls in your school decide to form a club. Do they have the right to keep boys from joining? The question may sound simple, but it is really very complicated—and very important. It involves the issue of freedom of association.

One of the first cases involving freedom of association to reach the Supreme Court was in 1988. The case involved large social clubs in New York City that limited membership to men. The clubs even refused to allow women to eat in their public restaurants. The city passed a law saying that large clubs could not discriminate against women. The clubs appealed to the courts, and insisted that the First Amendment allowed them to choose who they would allow to assemble in their buildings.

The "Million Man March"

In October 1995, Washington, D.C., was the scene of one of the largest demonstrations in the nation's history. The "Million Man March," organized by Nation of Islam leader Louis Farrakhan, was made up largely of African-American men and boys.

The event was a call to all African-American men to dedicate themselves to making life better in their families, neighborhoods, and communities. The gathering was criticized because Farrakhan excluded many groups of people, but it is a good example of Americans exercising their right to peaceably assemble. It is estimated that the day-long demonstration involved more than 400,000 people.

Thousands of men gathered on the Mall for the "Million Man March."

The Supreme Court ruled against the men's clubs. The justices said that when a club is so large that it operates restaurants and rents out facilities, it is no longer a private social group; instead, it is a public place and therefore cannot discriminate. Only small social gatherings have the freedom of association to limit membership.

The issue was raised again in 1993 when Louis Farrakhan, leader of the African-American Nation of Islam, rented an auditorium in Boston, Massachusetts, for a speech. The plan caused controversy for two reasons. First, Farrakhan would allow only African-American men into the auditorium. Did Farrakhan have the right to exclude whites and African-American women from this assembly? Second, many of Farrakhan's previous speeches had included vicious attacks against American Jews, raising fears that the Nation of Islam leader planned to stir up anti-Jewish sentiment in his audience.

Although no court case was involved, city officials asked a federal judge for an opinion. The judge stated that Farrakhan was within his constitutional rights to place limits on who could attend the meeting. And, in his speech, he was free to say anything he wanted, as long as he did not incite his audience to break the law.

Louis Farrakhan leads the Nation of Islam in America.

Boston was the scene of another debated case in 1995, when an organization of gay men applied for a permit to join an Independence Day parade. The march was planned by a war veterans' group that did not want participation by the gays because they were afraid that the event would turn into a rally for gay rights. When the permit was denied, the gay organization took the case to the courts, arguing that their members had a First Amendment right to participate in the parade. The march organizers argued that their right

to freedom of association allowed them the freedom to assemble with groups and individuals of their own choosing.

The Supreme Court ruled in favor of the march organizers. The justices said that the veterans' group had the right to limit this assembling of people to groups that supported the main purpose of the march. The courts have now ruled on several other freedom of association cases. But it seems that more Supreme Court decisions will be needed to establish how far organizations can go in limiting participation.

Special-interest groups, such as this gay rights group, are challenging many established practices of assembly.

• Under the Constitution, every American is empowered to express his or her views and take action on things they believe in.

Chapter 4

FREEDOM OF ASSEMBLY
AND THE INDIVIDUAL

Eleanor Roosevelt, the wife of President Franklin D. Roosevelt, was one of America's great champions of individual rights. After her husband's death in 1945, she was a major figure in creating the United Nations Declaration of Human Rights.

Where do our rights begin? Mrs. Roosevelt once asked in a speech. This is how she answered her own question:

Our rights begin in small places, close to home—so close and so small that they cannot be seen on any maps of the world. Yet they are the world of the individual—our neighborhoods, our schools, our places of work. Such are the places where every man, woman and child seeks equal justice, equal opportunity, equal dignity without discrimination. Unless these rights have meaning there, they have little meaning anywhere.

In other words, each individual has a responsibility to keep alive the meaning of freedom in the "small places" in which we live. This sense of responsibility includes respecting the rights of others. The meaning of freedom is diminished if one person insists that his or her rights are somehow more important than the rights of others.

Here is an example: During a 1995 speech concerning the AIDS epidemic, President Bill Clinton was frequently interrupted by the shouts of a small group who felt that the government was not doing enough to help the victims of AIDS. No one would deny that these demonstrators had a right to assemble and petition the government. However, by their heckling, they were insisting that their rights were more important than the rights of the president and the people in the audience.

Taking Responsibility

Young people enjoy essentially the same liberties as adults. These rights, however, including freedom of assembly, are subject to certain limitations. Students in school cannot exercise personal liberties in any way that interferes with others' education. A group of students could not hold a demonstration during school hours, for example, because it would disrupt classes and interfere with the rights of others to learn. Students who feel they have a grievance can assemble to discuss the issue as long as the meeting has the approval of school officials.

Suppose a group of students wanted to demonstrate on school grounds after regular school hours. Would this be a constitutional exercise of freedom of assembly, or could

they legally be stopped by school officials? The courts have generally allowed the schools and the local community to decide such questions.

For example, a group of girls in a Detroit high school were upset because school budget cuts had forced the cancellation of intramural sports for girls, but the boys' football team was unaffected. At one game, about twenty girls marched around the football field carrying signs of protest. The school principal asked them to stop. When some refused, they were escorted off the field by security guards. The family of one girl tried to sue the school for violation of her First Amendment rights, but the case was dismissed. The judge ruled that the game was a school function, and school officials had the authority to decide what kind of behavior was disruptive or contrary to school policy. In this case, the girls had a right to protest, but they also had the responsibility to hold their demonstration in an appropriate manner.

A group of schoolchildren gathers to protest school budget cuts by Congress.

The importance of accepting responsibility in the exercise of free assembly is not limited to school life, as the following case shows. A group of teenagers in Los Angeles often gathered in the driveway of one boy's home. They stayed late into the night, talking loudly, playing the radio at high volume, and sometimes insulting passersby. After more than a year of complaints and visits by police officers, one neighbor took the case to court. The neighbor charged that the teens violated a city ordinance that stated that it was against the law for "any gathering of people to create loud, unnecessary and unusual noise, or to disturb the peace and quiet of any neighborhood."

The boy's parents challenged the city's law, arguing that it does not state clearly what constituted a violation. The judge did not agree. He said that the law relied on the "common sense" of people. The judge also told the boy and his parents that, while "young people have a right to assemble in a peaceful manner...they also have a responsibility to live in...harmony with their neighbors" by respecting the neighbors' rights.

How we exercise our rights and responsibilities often has little to do with court cases or the wording of the Constitution. In 1991, the senior class of a Chicago high school held a meeting to make plans for their graduation ceremonies and their senior prom. Students were invited to suggest songs they wanted the band to play at the prom. A dance committee would make the final selection. When the committee announced its list, however, a bitter debate erupted. African-American seniors saw that none of the songs they asked for were selected.

The white seniors, who made up about 80 percent of the class, defended the committee's choices. "It's just a case of the majority rules," one student argued. White students urged their black classmates not to destroy the class sense of unity. But the African-American students refused to give in. Thirty black students organized their own prom, separate from the rest of their class.

The solution of holding two proms was a sad ending. Both groups were right in their exercise of freedom of assembly and association. But they had somehow lost the deeper meaning of freedom that was intended to bring our people together instead of drive them apart.

In a television interview, Senator Paul Simon of Illinois was asked what

Incidents involving teens gathered in public places have spurred debate about the line between peaceful assembly and disturbing the peace.

young people could do to keep our basic freedoms as strong as possible. Senator Simon answered: "They can defend people who are members of any minority group, or who have ideas that are opposed by the majority. That is the real safeguard. The courts cannot make the Bill of Rights meaningful if a majority refuses to let any minority express its views, or assemble peaceably, or petition the government." He explained that, even if we do not respect a group's ideas, we can tolerate their right to hold viewpoints, however unpopular. "We have built a tradition of respect for liberties," Simon concluded. "We have to make sure these liberties are expanded so that everyone can take advantage of them."

Understanding the Bill of Rights

★ ★ ★ ★ ★ ★ ★ ★ ★ ★ ★ ★ ★ ★ ★ ★ ★ ★ ★

In 1791, the Bill of Rights became part of the U.S. Constitution. What are these rights and why are they important for us?

The First Amendment says that the government cannot interfere with people's rights to freedom of speech, freedom of the press, freedom of religion, and freedom of assembly. It also gives people the right to petition their leaders.

The Second Amendment says because a "well-regulated militia" is "necessary to the security of a free state," the government can't interfere with the people's right to "keep and bear arms." Arms are guns and other weapons.

At the time the Bill of Rights was written, most men still belonged to their local state militia, or army. They kept their guns at home so they could be ready to defend their country at a moment's notice.

Some people say that because we have no such state militia today, the Second Amendment doesn't give people the right to own guns. But other people say that the Second Amendment guarantees the right to own guns for many purposes, including defense of home and family.

The Third Amendment says that, except in time of war, troops cannot be lodged in private homes without the permission of homeowners. This was included because many people remembered a time when the British had forced citizens to open their homes to soldiers.

The Fourth Amendment says that people's homes and possessions can't be searched or taken without an official paper called a *warrant*. A warrant is a document, signed by a judge, that allows police to search for evidence of a crime. The amendment also says that a warrant cannot be issued without "*probable cause*." This means that the police must convince a judge that the search of a specific place is likely to produce evidence of a crime.

The Fifth Amendment protects people who are accused of crimes. It says that for a serious crime, such as murder, a person must be charged with the crime by a group called a grand jury. Twelve to twenty-three people make up a grand jury. They must examine the evidence that the government has against the person and then determine whether there is a strong enough case to charge the person with a crime.

The Fifth Amendment also says that a person can't be tried twice for the same crime and doesn't have to testify against himself or herself. In a trial, when someone who is on trial refuses to answer questions on the witness stand, we say the witness "takes the fifth."

Another important part of the Fifth Amendment says that no person can be "deprived of life, liberty, or property, without due process of law." This part of the amendment guarantees all citizens the right to a fair trial before they can be executed, put in prison, or have property taken away from them. It also means that any laws made in the United States must result in fair treatment of all citizens.

Last, the Fifth Amendment says that the government can't take anyone's property for public use without paying a fair price for it.

The Sixth Amendment gives people who are accused of crimes the right to a speedy and public trial by a jury of people from the area where the crime was committed. Without the right to a speedy trial, people could be arrested for crimes and stay in jail for years without ever having the chance to defend themselves in court. The amendment also says that those accused of crimes have the right to know their accusers, to be confronted by the people who have accused them, and to have a lawyer defend them.

The Seventh Amendment gives people involved in lawsuits over money or property the right to trial by a jury. It also says that once a decision is made by that jury, the decision can't be changed unless it can be shown that the trial was flawed in some way.

The Eighth Amendment protects people who are put in jail. The first part of the amendment says that a judge cannot require "excessive bail" for someone accused of a crime. Bail is money that a person must pay to be freed from jail during the time before a trial begins. The money is returned after a person shows up for trial.

The Eighth Amendment also says that no one can be given "cruel and unusual punishment" for a crime. If a person were convicted of stealing a loaf of bread, for example, it would be cruel and unusual punishment to sentence that person to ten years in jail. The rule against cruel and unusual punishment also prevents such things as the torture of prisoners.

The Ninth Amendment says that the fact that some rights are not specifically mentioned does not mean that the people do not have them.

The Tenth Amendment says that any powers not given to the government by the Constitution belong to the states and the people. This amendment was very important to people at the time the Bill of Rights was ratified. Many people still feared a large, powerful national government, and this amendment put limits on the government.

The Bill of Rights gave citizens of the United States many freedoms and protections that few people in other parts of the world had.

Glossary

★ ★ ★ ★ ★ ★

bill of rights A list of individual rights or freedoms that cannot be taken away by the government. The first ten amendments to the U.S. Constitution make up the U.S. Bill of Rights. Most state constitutions also include a bill of rights.

declaration Any formal statement or announcement, such as the Declaration of Independence.

demonstration A public gathering, rally, or march designed to show a group's opinion on an important issue.

freedom of association The courts have interpreted freedom of assembly to include freedom of association —the right of people to choose whom they will assemble with, and to exclude others.

grievance A complaint, a problem, or a feeling of injustice. When people feel they have been wronged, they have a grievance against others or against the government.

petition Usually a formal, written request, or appeal, to a government or a court of law. Public demonstrations have sometimes been called "living petitions."

redress A correction of a wrong, or a solution to a problem.

★ ★ ★ ★ ★ ★ ★ ★ ★ ★ ★ ★

Bray, Rosemary L. *Martin Luther King.* New York: Greenwillow Books, 1995.

Coleman, Warren. *The Bill of Rights.* Chicago: Children's Press, 1989.

Fradin, Dennis B. *The Declaration of Independence.* Chicago: Children's Press, 1988.

Goldish, Meish. *Our Supreme Court.* Brookfield, CT: The Millbrook Press, 1994.

Johnson, Linda Carlson. *Our Constitution.* Brookfield, CT: The Millbrook Press, 1992.

King, David C. *First Facts About U. S. History.* Woodbridge, CT: Blackbirch Press, 1996.

Oneal, Zibby. *A Long Way to Go: A Story of Women's Right to Vote.* New York: Viking Children's Books, 1990.

Schleifer, Jay. *Our Declaration of Independence.* Brookfield, CT: The Millbrook Press, 1992.

Stein, R. Conrad. *The Bill of Rights.* Chicago: Children's Press, 1992.

Wade, Linda R. *Montgomery: Launching the Civil Rights Movement.* Vero Beach, FL: Rourke Enterprises, 1991.

Index

★ ★ ★ ★